cookies

PEGGY PORSCHEN

PHOTOGRAPHY BY
GEORGIA GLYNN SMITH

Quadrille
PUBLISHING

'To my two boys, Bryn & Max xx'

Contents

Baking Hints & Tips

INGREDIENTS

• For best results, use good-quality ingredients, such as free-range eggs, proper unsalted butter (not margarine) and good-quality extracts (not essences).

• All your ingredients should be at room temperature unless the recipe states otherwise. If needed, you can use the defrost setting on the microwave to gently soften the butter, and uncracked whole eggs can be gently warmed in a bowl of tepid water for 10 minutes.

KNEADING & ROLLING DOUGH

• Always roll cookie dough from chilled for best results.

• Before rolling, give the dough a quick knead to soften it. Do not overwork your dough and never re-roll more than once as it will toughen up.

• Use as little flour as possible when rolling out the dough as otherwise it will become dry and brittle.

• For an even thickness use marzipan spacers or guide sticks.

• Always bake your cookies from chilled to prevent them from spreading, or even from frozen for best results.

CUTTING SHAPES

• Use cookie cutters to cut your cookie shapes out, if more specialist cookie cutters are required visit peggyporschen.com. Alternatively, create cardboard templates for the cookies using the dimensions given in each recipe.

TIMINGS & TEMPERATURES

• These are only guidelines. Bear in mind that ovens can vary greatly in their accuracy. The temperatures stated are for conventional ovens, so you will need to lower the temperature by 10–15°C if using a fan-assisted oven.

• Always bake cookies of the same size together on a tray, otherwise the smaller ones will burn while the large ones are baking.

• Turn the trays around halfway through cooking to ensure even baking. Move swiftly to avoid losing heat in your oven.

DRYING & HUMIDITY

• Royal icing can take longer to dry in humid weather conditions. Speed up the drying

process by placing iced cookies in a warm oven (at approximately 80°C) for about half an hour. If you decorate lots of cookies on a regular basis, it is worth buying a dehumidifier for your kitchen.

• Grease patches may occasionally appear in paler coloured icing. This is usually because the environment is too humid or the cookies overheated when drying in the oven, causing the fat to seep out of the butter and mark the cookies. The colour may even out after a few days, but to prevent this from happening again, glaze un-iced cookies with a thin layer of boiled sieved apricot jam. Once dry, ice the cookies as you normally would.

• Humid or damp conditions can make cookies go soft. But if the air is too dry, the icing can fall off. It is therefore important to store cookies in airtight containers or wrap them in cling film.

• Gingerbread cookies can get soggy if left out too long in humid conditions. If they do start to lose firmness, flush them through the oven at around 100°C until they feel crisp again.

STORAGE & SHELF LIFE

• Cookie dough or uncooked cookies can be wrapped in cling film and stored in the freezer for up to 3 months. Cookies baked from frozen hold their shape better in the oven as they don't tend to spread out as much as chilled ones.

• If stored in an airtight container, baked sugar cookies will keep for up to 1 month and baked gingerbread cookies will keep up to 3 months.

• You can tell if cookies have gone off by the smell. They begin to smell of stale, rancid butter.

PREPARING COOKIES

• Make ribbon holes for hanging cookies only when the royal icing is completely dry, otherwise it will crack. Use a small electric drill with a clean, sterilised drill bit (about 3–4mm in diameter). Place the cookies on a wire rack, then holding the electric drill vertically, make a small hole in the top of each cookie. Alternatively, while the cookies are still hot, use a tiny round cookie cutter or the tip of a long, thin piping nozzle to make the ribbon holes. As the cookies are hot, take care not to burn your fingers when using this method.

• To make cookie pops, roll out the cookie dough until about 4–5mm thick. Use a cutter to cut out the cookies, then insert a cookie or a cake pop stick about halfway into the side of each cookie. Patch the back of the cookie up with some extra dough if required. Bake as normal.

Vanilla Cookies

MAKES 25 MEDIUM OR 12 LARGE COOKIES

INGREDIENTS

200g unsalted butter, softened

200g caster sugar

Seeds of 1 vanilla pod or 1 tbsp vanilla extract

A pinch of salt

1 medium egg, lightly beaten

400g plain flour, plus extra for dusting

Line 2 baking trays with greaseproof paper.

Place the butter, sugar, vanilla and salt in a bowl and cream together. Do not overwork the mixture, or the cookies will spread during baking.

Beat the egg in a jug and slowly add to the butter mixture, whisking until well incorporated. Sift in the flour and mix until just combined. Gather the dough into a ball, wrap in cling film and chill for at least 30 minutes.

Place the dough on a lightly floured surface and briefly knead. Roll out the dough, until about 4–5mm thick (unless stated otherwise).

Use cookie cutters to cut out the desired shapes and place the cookies onto prepared baking trays. Chill again for about 30 minutes, or until cool and firm. Meanwhile, preheat the oven to 175°C/Gas mark 3.

Bake the cookies for 6–10 minutes, or until the edges are golden brown. Leave to cool completely on a wire rack.

FLAVOUR VARIATIONS

Lemon
Omit the vanilla and add the finely grated zest of 1 lemon.

Chocolate
Omit the vanilla and replace 50g of the plain flour with 50g cocoa powder.

Gingerbread Cookies

MAKES 40 MEDIUM OR 20 LARGE COOKIES

INGREDIENTS

5 tbsp water

210g light brown sugar

3 tbsp treacle

3 tbsp golden syrup

3 tbsp ground ginger

3 tbsp ground cinnamon

1 tsp ground cloves

250g salted butter, cold and diced

1 tsp bicarbonate of soda

560g plain flour, plus extra for dusting

Line 4 baking trays with greaseproof paper.

Place the water, brown sugar, treacle, golden syrup, ground ginger, cinnamon and cloves in a deep saucepan. Bring the mixture to the boil over a medium heat, stirring continuously.

Remove from the heat and gradually add the diced butter. Stir until combined. Add the bicarbonate of soda – take care as the mixture will swell up. Leave to cool to room temperature.

Once cool, transfer the mixture to a large bowl. Sift in the flour and slowly mix together to form a slightly wet and sticky dough. Wrap in cling film and chill for 2 hours, or until cool and firm.

Place the dough on a lightly floured surface and roll it out, until about 5–6mm thick (unless stated otherwise).

Use cookie cutters to cut out the desired shapes and place the cookies onto prepared baking trays. Chill again for at least 30 minutes. Meanwhile, preheat the oven to 200°C/Gas mark 6.

Bake the cookies for 8–10 minutes, or until they spring back to the touch and the edges are slightly darkened. Leave to cool completely on a wire rack.

Graphic Print Tiles

INGREDIENTS

1 batch vanilla cookies (see page 8) in the shape of plaques (8 x 8cm)

500g royal icing (see page 56)

Green, blue, pink, yellow and black food colours

SPECIAL EQUIPMENT

Geometric stencils available from Peggy Porschen or you can make your own (see page 62)

First prepare your paper piping bags (see page 57). Adjust the consistency of your royal icing (see pages 58 and 60). You will need 1 bag of white soft-peak icing and 1 bag of white flooding icing. Once prepared, keep the piping bags in a re-sealable plastic bag to prevent the icing from drying out between use.

Take the piping bag filled with soft-peak icing and cut a small section from the tip of the piping bag. Trace the border of the cookie, then use the flooding icing to fill the outlined area. Leave the icing to dry completely.

Meanwhile, divide the remaining royal icing into sixths, keep 1 bag of white soft-peak icing for decoration and colour the rest (see page 56) with green, blue, pink, yellow and pale grey (using black food colour). Adjust the consistency to soft-peak and keep the icing in separate bowls covered with a clean damp cloth to prevent them from drying out.

Stencil a fifth of your cookies (see page 62) using green soft-peak icing. Repeat for the remaining cookies, using the other royal icing colours and stencil designs. Make sure to clean the stencils between each use.

Once the cookies are dry, pipe an outline around the border of the plaques with some white soft-peak icing.

Sweet Heart Cookie Pops

INGREDIENTS

1 batch vanilla cookie dough (see page 8) in the shape of a scalloped circle (8cm diameter), using the technique for cookie pops

Plain flour, for dusting

Cookie or cake pop sticks

500g royal icing (see page 56)

Pink and red food colours

50g florist paste

Small amount of white vegetable fat

Edible glue

SPECIAL EQUIPMENT

Small heart cutter

First prepare your cookie pops (see page 7).

Then prepare your paper piping bags (see page 57). Adjust the colour (see page 56) and consistency of your royal icing (see pages 58 and 60). You will need 1 bag of pale pink soft-peak icing, 1 bag of white soft-peak icing and 1 bag of pale pink flooding icing. Once prepared, keep the piping bags in a re-sealable plastic bag to prevent the icing from drying out between use.

Take the piping bag filled with pale pink soft-peak icing and cut a small section from the tip of the piping bag. Pipe the outline of a circle just within the scalloped edge of the cookies. Fill the outlined areas with pale pink flooding icing and leave the cookies to dry completely.

Meanwhile, knead the florist paste until smooth and pliable, adding a small amount of vegetable fat if it feels hard and brittle. Knead in some red food colour, then roll out the paste until about 1mm thick. Use a small heart cutter to cut out hearts and adhere them to the centre of the cookies with edible glue.

Finally, use white soft-peak icing to pipe dots on each scallop and around the florist paste hearts.

Fluttering Butterflies

MAKES 6 OF EACH SIZE

INGREDIENTS

1 batch chocolate cookies (see page 8) in the shapes of butterflies, (cut in half before baking): small (6cm), medium (9cm) and large (12cm) or cutters available from Peggy Porschen

500g royal icing (see page 56)

Brown, green, orange, purple, pink, blue and yellow food colours

SPECIAL EQUIPMENT

Cupcake cases (non-stick)

TIP

To make a turquoise shade, mix a little bit of yellow with blue food colouring.

First prepare your paper piping bags (see page 57). Adjust the colour (see page 56) and consistency of your royal icing (see pages 58 and 60). You will need 1 bag of brown stiff-peak icing, 1 bag of brown soft-peak icing and 1 bag of flooding icing in each colour (green, orange, purple, pink, yellow and turquoise). Once prepared, keep the piping bags in a re-sealable plastic bag to prevent the icing from drying out between use.

Take the piping bag filled with brown soft-peak icing, cut a small section from the tip of the piping bag and pipe the outlines of the butterfly wings. Fill the outlined areas with flooding icing in the colour of your choice. While still wet, pipe a different colour of flooding icing into the centre of the wings. Outline each inner section with a third, contrasting colour of flooding icing. Use only 2 colours for the smallest butterflies.

To make the feather design, pull a cocktail stick through the wet icing, moving it from the edge towards the centre of the wing. For flat dots, drop dots of flooding icing into the freshly flooded cookie. Leave the icing to dry completely.

To finish the cookies, use brown stiff-peak royal icing to make the butterfly bodies. In a cupcake case, pipe a long section of stiff-peak icing into the middle and then stick two wings on each side, resting the wings on the sides of the cupcake case. Snip a slightly larger hole at the top of the piping bag and pipe a body between the wings, creating a teardrop shape that narrows towards the bottom. Then pipe a large dot above the teardrop for the head. Leave the icing to dry for a couple of hours.

Sailing Boats

MAKES 20

INGREDIENTS

1 batch vanilla cookies (see page 8) in the shape of sailing boats (8 x 10cm)

500g royal icing (see page 56)

Blue, red and black food colours

First prepare your paper piping bags (see page 57). Adjust the colour (see page 56) and consistency of your royal icing (see pages 58 and 60). You will need soft-peak pale grey icing and both soft-peak and flooding consistencies of white, pale blue, dark blue and red royal icing. Once prepared, keep the piping bags in a re-sealable plastic bag to prevent the icing from drying out between use.

Take a piping bag filled with soft-peak icing, cut a small section from the tip of the piping bag and pipe the outline of the hull on one of the cookies. Fill the outlined area with flooding icing of the same colour. Repeat for the remaining cookies, using all the colours of soft-peak and flooding icing. Leave them to dry completely.

Repeat the process to outline and flood the small rectangular section on top of the hulls with a contrasting colour of royal icing. Leave them to dry completely, then pipe on the decorative lines and dots with soft-peak icing.

Use pale grey soft-peak icing to pipe the masts vertically down the sails, from the top corner down to the hull. Outline the sails with white soft-peak icing, then fill them with white flooding icing. While still wet, pipe lines across the larger sails with pale blue, dark blue and red flooding icing. Leave them to dry completely.

To finish the cookies, use dark blue soft-peak icing to pipe numbers into the corners of the smaller sails.

Birthday Party

INGREDIENTS

1 batch vanilla cookies (see page 8) in the shape of squares (5 x 5cm) and tiered cakes (10 x 10cm)

500g royal icing (see page 56)

Blue, claret, pink and yellow food colours

TIP

You can decorate the cookie cakes with swags, lines, dots or any other pattern or write 'Happy Birthday' across the middle. For dots, thin down some soft-peak icing with a little water to avoid creating peaks.

First prepare your paper piping bags (see page 57). Adjust the colour (see page 56) and consistency of your royal icing (see pages 58 and 60). You will need both soft-peak and flooding consistencies of white, blue, claret, pink and yellow royal icing. Once prepared, keep the piping bags in a re-sealable plastic bag to prevent the icing from drying out between use.

Begin with the gift boxes. Take a piping bag filled with blue soft-peak icing, cut a small section from the tip of the piping bag and trace the outline of a square cookie. Fill the outlined area with blue flooding icing. While still wet, pipe diagonal lines across the square with a contrasting colour of flooding icing. Repeat this process for the remaining square cookies, but use the claret, pink and yellow icings to decorate them. Leave them to dry completely.

Once dry, pipe the ribbon onto the gift boxes, matching the ribbon colour to the diagonal stripes. First use soft-peak icing to pipe a cross centred in the middle, then pipe on the bow.

To decorate the birthday cakes, pipe the outlines of the cakes (2 tiers only) with white soft-peak royal icing. Fill the centres with white flooding icing and leave them to dry completely.

Once dry, pipe the white outline and lines marking the 2 tiers of the cake. Then use the coloured soft-peak icing to decorate the cakes. Finally, pipe candles in different colours on the top tier of the cake using soft-peak icing and finish them with yellow flames. Leave the icing to dry completely.

Balloons

MAKES 25

INGREDIENTS

1 batch vanilla cookies (see page 8) in the shape of balloons (7cm diameter)

500g royal icing (see page 56)

Blue, pink and yellow food colours

TIP

To decorate your balloons, use edible glue to stick a thin satin ribbon to the back of each of your balloon cookies.

First prepare your paper piping bags (see page 57). Adjust the colour (see page 56) and consistency of your royal icing (see pages 58 and 60). You will need both soft-peak and flooding consistencies of blue, pink and yellow royal icing, as well as 1 bag of white flooding icing. Once prepared, keep the piping bags in a re-sealable plastic bag to prevent the icing from drying out between use.

Take a piping bag filled with blue soft-peak icing and cut a small section from the tip of the piping bag. Trace the blue outlines of the balloons on a third of the cookies, then fill the outlined area with blue flooding icing. While still wet, drop a dot of white flooding icing near the top edge of the balloons. Run a cocktail stick through the white icing, following the curve of the balloon and pulling it into the blue icing to create an accent. This will give the balloon cookies a 3-dimensional effect.

Repeat for the remaining balloon cookies, decorating an equal number with the pink and yellow icing. Leave them to dry completely.

Floral Brush Embroidery

**MAKES 30 SMALL &
20 LARGE**

INGREDIENTS

1 batch vanilla cookies (see page 8) in the shape of 5-petal blossoms (5cm diameter)

1 batch gingerbread cookies (see page 59) in the shape of ovals with scalloped edges (12 x 8cm)

500g royal icing (see page 56)

Edible gold lustre

Small amount of vodka or lemon juice

Small amount of piping gel

SPECIAL EQUIPMENT

A fine paintbrush

TIP

If you want to create more definition with your brush strokes, dry the paintbrush in between your fingers, slightly flattening it. Then pull the paintbrush through the icing on the thinner edge.

First prepare your paper piping bag (see page 57). Adjust the consistency of your royal icing (see page 58). You will need white royal icing of soft-peak consistency. Once prepared, keep the piping bag in a re-sealable plastic bag to prevent the icing from drying out between use.

Begin with brush embroidery and piping for the blossom cookies (see page 63). Use the same method to pipe on the second layer of 5 smaller petals, arranging them evenly in between the petals of the first layer. Leave them to dry completely, then pipe a fine outline over the petal edges followed by the flower centres, which are made up of 1 dot surrounded by 6 dots.

Use the same brush embroidery technique to decorate the gingerbread oval cookies. However, these flowers are piped on in free-form and each is made up of 1 layer of 3–4 petals. Pipe a thin outline over the petal edges followed by 1 dot in the centres of smaller flowers and 4 dots for the larger flowers.

To embellish the flowers with gold lustre, mix together small amounts of lustre, vodka and piping gel to create a thick paste. Once the cookies are dry, use a fine paintbrush over the edges of the petals and the flower centres with the gold lustre paste.

Baby Grows

MAKES 25

INGREDIENTS

1 batch vanilla cookies (see page 8) in the shape of baby grows (7 x 10cm) or cutters available from Peggy Porschen

500g royal icing (see page 56)

Pink, blue, yellow and brown food colours

50g florist paste

Small amount of white vegetable fat

Edible glue (optional)

SPECIAL EQUIPMENT

Small cutters in the shapes of teddy bears, whales and ducks available from Peggy Porschen or any other shapes you prefer

TIP

Alternatively, you could leave some baby grows plain, use different colours of flooding icing for the stripes or even decorate them with dots of flooding icing.

Prepare your paper piping bags (see page 57). Adjust the colour (see page 56) and consistency of your royal icing (see pages 58 and 60). You will need both soft-peak and flooding consistencies of pale pink, pale blue, pale yellow and white royal icing, as well as 1 bag of brown soft-peak icing. Once prepared, keep the piping bags in a re-sealable plastic bag to prevent the icing from drying out between use.

Take a piping bag filled with pale pink soft-peak icing and cut a small section from the tip of the piping bag. Trace the outlines of the baby grows on a third of the cookies, then fill the outlined areas with pale pink flooding icing. While still wet, use white flooding icing to pipe horizontal lines across the cookies. Repeat for the remaining cookies, decorating an equal number with the blue and yellow icing. Leave to dry completely.

Meanwhile, knead the florist paste until smooth and pliable, adding a small amount of vegetable fat if it feels hard and brittle. Divide the paste into 3 parts and mix 1 part with blue food colour, 1 part with yellow food colour and 1 part with brown food colour. Roll out the coloured florist pastes, until about 1mm thick. Cut out teddy bears, whales and ducks (or any other shapes you prefer) with small cutters and adhere them to the cookies with edible glue or a dab of icing.

Pipe over the outlines of the baby grows and add the details of the suits with the corresponding colours of soft-peak icing. Use white soft-peak icing to pipe the 3 dots for the buttons. Finally, use brown, pink and yellow soft-peak icing to add details to the florist paste. You may need to transfer the icing to new piping bags and cut smaller holes in the tips to pipe thinner lines.

Gingerbread Men Jars

MAKES 20

INGREDIENTS

1 batch gingerbread cookies (see page 9) in the shape of cookie jars (8 x 12cm)

500g royal icing (see page 56)

Ivory, blue, red and brown food colours

100g florist paste

Small amount of white vegetable fat

Edible glue

SPECIAL EQUIPMENT

Small gingerbread man cutter

TIP
You can use the gingerbread cutters to cut out overlapping parts of the gingerbread men, so they fit together like puzzle pieces.

Prepare your paper piping bags (see page 57). Adjust the colour (see page 56) and consistency of your royal icing (see pages 58 and 60). You will need both soft-peak and flooding consistencies of ivory and light blue royal icing, as well as 1 bag of red and 1 white soft-peak icing. Once prepared, keep the piping bags in a re-sealable plastic bag to prevent the icing from drying out between use.

Take a piping bag filled with light blue soft-peak icing, cut a small section from the tip of the piping bag and trace the outline of the jar, leaving out the lid part of the cookie. Fill the outlined area with light blue flooding icing. Repeat for the remaining cookies and leave them to dry completely.

Once dry, use ivory soft-peak icing to trace the outlines of the jar lids and then fill them with ivory flooding icing. Leave them to dry completely.

Meanwhile, knead the florist paste until smooth and pliable, adding a small amount of white vegetable fat if it feels hard and brittle. Knead in some brown food colour and roll out the paste, until about 1mm thick. Cut out gingerbread men with the small cutter – you will need 3 for each cookie. Adhere the gingerbread men to the cookies with edible glue.

Pipe the outlines and details of the jar lids with ivory soft-peak icing. Then pipe the outlines of the jars with light blue soft-peak icing, adding details to give them a more 3-dimensional effect. To finish the cookies, use red soft-peak icing to pipe bows onto the gingerbread men and white soft-peak icing to pipe on their faces and buttons.

Clouds & Hot Air Balloons

MAKES 10 OF EACH

INGREDIENTS

1 batch vanilla cookies (see page 8) in the shape of hot air balloons (8 x 10cm) and clouds (9 x 7cm)

500g royal icing (see page 56)

Brown, purple, pink, mint and blue food colours

SPECIAL EQUIPMENT

Cloud stencils available from Peggy Porschen or you can make your own (see page 62)

Small electric drill with 3mm drill bit for food use only

A selection of thin satin ribbons

Prepare your paper piping bags (see page 57). Adjust the colour (see page 56) and consistency of your royal icing (see pages 58 and 60). You will need both soft-peak and flooding consistencies of light brown, purple, pink, mint and blue royal icing. Once prepared, keep the piping bags in a re-sealable plastic bag to prevent the icing from drying out between use.

Take a piping bag filled with light brown soft-peak icing, cut a small section from the tip of the piping bag and trace the outline of the baskets on all of the balloon cookies. Fill the outlined areas with light brown flooding icing. Use purple soft-peak icing to trace the outlines of the balloons on a third of the cookies. Fill the outlined areas with purple flooding icing. Repeat for the remaining cookies, decorating an equal number with pink and mint icing. Leave them to dry completely.

Once dry, use light brown soft-peak icing to pipe the outlines and cross-hatch patterns on the baskets. Next, pipe the swag details across the middle of the balloons and leave to dry. Then pipe the outlines and details on the balloon sections of the cookies, matching the colours to the flooding icing. Finally, pipe on the bows and dots with a different colour of soft-peak icing.

To decorate the cloud cookies, first pipe the outlines with white soft-peak icing. Fill the outlined areas with white flooding icing and leave them to dry completely. Colour some white royal icing with blue food colour and adjust the consistency to soft-peak. Keep it in a bowl covered with a clean damp cloth to prevent it from drying out. Using your cloud stencil, stencil your cloud cookies (see page 62). Finally, make the ribbon holes (see page 7) and thread coloured ribbons through all of your cookies.

Easter Eggs

INGREDIENTS

1 batch chocolate cookies (see page 8) in the shape of eggs (4 x 7cm)

500g royal icing (see page 56)

Claret, orange, green and yellow food colours

Prepare your paper piping bags (see page 57). Adjust the colour (see page 56) and consistency of your royal icing (see pages 58 and 60). You will need both soft-peak and flooding consistencies of pale pink (using a little claret), peach, (using orange with a little claret), coral pink (using claret with a little orange), green and yellow icing. Once prepared, keep the piping bags in a re-sealable plastic bag to prevent the icing from drying out between use.

Take a piping bag filled with pale pink soft-peak icing, cut a small section from the tip of the piping bag and pipe the outline of a strip about 5mm wide vertically down the middle of an egg-shaped cookie. Pipe another strip of the same width to bisect the first one, slightly curving it upwards. Fill the outlined areas with pink flooding icing. Repeat for the remaining cookies, decorating an equal number with the peach, coral pink, green and yellow icing. Leave them to dry completely.

Once dry, use corresponding colours of soft-peak icing to pipe outlines for the bows, centring them over the intersection of the 2 ribbons. Fill the bows with flooding icing and leave them to dry.

To finish the cookies, pipe over the outlines of the bows with soft-peak royal icing and dot the centres with flooding icing.

Groomsmen

MAKES 14

INGREDIENTS

1 batch vanilla cookies (see page 8) in the shape of tuxedos (8 x 10cm) or groom cutters available from Peggy Porschen

500g royal icing (see page 56)

Black, pink and orange food colours

Prepare your paper piping bags (see page 57). Adjust the colour (see page 56) and consistency of your royal icing (see pages 58 and 60). You will need both soft-peak and flooding consistencies of pale grey (using black), pale pink and white royal icing, as well as 1 bag of dark grey and peach (using pink and orange) soft-peak icing. Once prepared, keep the piping bags in a re-sealable plastic bag to prevent the icing from drying out between use.

Take a piping bag filled with pale grey soft-peak icing, cut a small section from the tip of the piping bag and pipe the outlines of the waistcoats. Then use white soft-peak icing to outline the necks and sleeves of the shirts. Fill the outlined waistcoats with pale grey flooding icing and leave them to dry. Once dry, fill the necks and sleeves of the shirts with white flooding icing. Leave them to dry completely.

Once dry, use pale grey soft-peak icing to outline the waistcoats and pipe 3 pockets onto each cookie. Outline the shirts, collars and cuffs with white soft-peak icing. Outline the ties with soft-peak icing and fill the ties with pale pink flooding icing and leave them to dry.

To finish the cookies, use dark grey soft-peak icing to add buttons to the waistcoats and shirts, and pipe stripes on the ties with peach soft-peak icing.

Bridesmaids

MAKES 12

INGREDIENTS

1 batch vanilla cookies (see page 8) in the shape of prom dresses (9 x 12cm) or bride cutters available from Peggy Porschen

500g royal icing (see page 56)

Orange, pink and yellow food colours

Small edible sugar blossoms (you can either make your own or buy them in the supermarket or from sugarcraft suppliers)

Prepare your paper piping bags (see page 57). Adjust the colour (see page 56) and consistency of your royal icing (see pages 58 and 60). You will need both soft-peak and flooding consistencies of peach (made with orange and pink food colour), pale yellow and pale pink royal icing, as well as 1 bag of white soft-peak icing. Once prepared, keep the piping bags in a re-sealable plastic bag to prevent the icing from drying out between use.

Take a piping bag filled with peach soft-peak icing, cut a small section from the tip of the piping bag and pipe the outlines of the prom dresses on a third of the cookies, then fill them with peach flooding icing. Repeat for the remaining cookies, decorating an equal number with the pale yellow and pale pink icing. Leave them to dry completely.

Once dry, pipe belts and ribbons onto the dresses with the soft-peak icings. To finish the cookies, use soft-peak icing to adhere the edible sugar blossoms to the cookies.

Ice Cream Cones

INGREDIENTS

1 batch vanilla cookies (see page 8) in the shape of ice creams (5 x 10cm)

500g royal icing (see page 56)

Ivory, yellow, peach, pink and blue food colours

Hundreds & Thousands

Multicoloured sugar sprinkles

TIP

You could also pipe some flooding icing dripping down onto the cone, so the ice cream appears to be melting.

Prepare your paper piping bags (see page 57). Adjust the colour (see page 56) and consistency of your royal icing (see pages 58 and 60). You will need both soft-peak and flooding consistencies of pale brown (using lots of ivory), yellow, peach, pink, blue and cream (using a little ivory) royal icing. Once prepared, keep the piping bags in a re-sealable plastic bag to prevent the icing from drying out between use.

Take a piping bag filled with pale brown soft-peak icing, cut a small section from the tip of the piping bag and pipe the outlines of the cones. Fill the outlined sections with pale brown flooding icing and leave them to dry completely.

Once dry, pipe a cross-hatch pattern over the cones with the pale brown soft-peak icing.

Take a piping bag filled with yellow soft-peak icing, cut a small section from the tip of the bag and pipe outlines for the ice cream part on a fifth of the cookies. Fill the outlined areas with yellow flooding icing. Repeat for the remaining cookies, decorating an equal number with the peach, pink, blue and cream icings.

Leave the cookies to set slightly, then sprinkle the tops with Hundreds & Thousands and multicoloured sugar sprinkles. Leave them to dry completely.

Tiered Cakes

INGREDIENTS

1 batch chocolate cookie dough (see page 8) 12 squares each: small (4 x 4cm), medium (6 x 6cm) and large (8 x 8cm) cutters

Plain flour, for dusting

500g royal icing (see page 56)

Pink food colour

Pink edible sugar blossoms (you can either make your own or buy them in the supermarket or from sugarcraft suppliers)

Prepare the dough and roll it out until about 3mm thick, then cut into squares with small, medium and large square cutters. You will need 4 cookies of each size for each tiered cake. Then bake as normal (see page 8).

Colour the royal icing with pink food colour, making it slightly darker than the sugar blossoms. Adjust the consistency of the pink icing, adding water until it is soft-peak (see page 58) and prepare a paper piping bag (see page 57). Once prepared, keep the piping bags in a re-sealable plastic bag to prevent the icing from drying out between use.

To assemble the bottom tier, snip a small section off the front of the piping bag and pipe an outline of about 3mm thickness around the edges of 3 of the largest squares. Place them evenly on top of one another and finish with the fourth plain cookie on top. Use enough icing to create some height and so it just shows at the edges of the cookies, but not too much that it begins to run down the side of the cake. Repeat the stacking and layering of the cookies to assemble the top 2 tiers, each made of 4 cookies. Then assemble each section together with pink soft-peak icing.

Use the icing to adhere the edible sugar blossoms to the tiered cake, placing a small bouquet of the blossoms on the top of the cake, as well as several down the sides.

Retro Teapots

MAKES 20

INGREDIENTS

1 batch vanilla cookie (see page 8) in various teapot shapes: blue (9 x 9cm), pink (7 x 10cm), green (7 x 10cm) and yellow (10 x 10cm) or cutters available from Peggy Porschen

500g royal icing (see page 56)

Blue, pink, green and yellow food colours

First prepare your paper piping bags (see page 57). Adjust the colour (see page 56) and consistency of your royal icing (see pages 58 and 60). You will need both soft-peak and flooding consistencies of blue, pink, green and yellow royal icing. Once prepared, keep the piping bags in a re-sealable plastic bag to prevent the icing from drying out between use.

Take a piping bag filled with blue soft-peak icing, cut a small section from the tip of the piping bag and trace the outlines of the teapots on a quarter of the cookies. Fill the outlined area with blue flooding icing. Repeat for the remaining cookies, decorating an equal number with the pink, yellow and green royal icing. Leave them to dry completely.

Once dry, pipe outlines and decorative details onto the cookies using soft-peak icing, matching the colours to the flooding icing.

Orchid Blossoms

INGREDIENTS

1 batch vanilla cookies (see page 8) in small rounds (3.5cm diameter)

100g sugar paste

100g florist paste

Small amount of white vegetable fat

Green and purple food colours

Purple and yellow petal dust

Edible glue

100g royal icing (see page 56)

SPECIAL EQUIPMENT

Silicone orchid mould (from Peggy Porschen)

A fine paintbrush

Edible purple food colour pen

Dresden tool or small kitchen knife

Knead together the sugar paste and florist paste until smooth and pliable, adding a small amount of white vegetable fat if it feels hard and brittle. Mix about 25g of the paste with green food colour to a pale green shade and knead a small amount of purple food colour into the remaining paste to make a light purple shade. Cover both pastes with cling film and leave it to rest for about 30 minutes.

Rub a thin layer of white vegetable fat over the silicone mould. Press a hazelnut-sized piece of purple paste firmly into the mould. Smooth the surface and clean up the edges with your fingers. Carefully bend the mould outwards to release the flower.

Leave the flowers to set, then brush the edges of the petals with purple petal dust. Use an edible pen to add dark purple dots to the petals.

Shape a small oval bud for each orchid centre from the pale green paste, then gently score them vertically down the middle with the thin end of a Dresden tool. Attach the buds onto the orchids, by adding edible glue into the centre of the orchid and attaching the bud to it. Leave to dry completely and then brush with yellow dust.

Pipe a small amount of royal icing onto each cookie and then stick on a finished orchid.

Cupcakes

MAKES 30

INGREDIENTS

1 batch vanilla cookies (see page 8) in the shape of mini cupcakes (5 x 5cm)

500g royal icing (see page 56)

Brown, yellow, pink and blue food colours

Multicoloured sugar sprinkles

Prepare your paper piping bags (see page 57). Adjust the colour (see page 56) and consistency of your royal icing (see pages 58 and 60). You will need both soft-peak and flooding consistencies of brown, yellow, pale pink, dark pink, blue and white royal icing. Once prepared, keep the piping bags in a re-sealable plastic bag to prevent the icing from drying out between use.

Take a piping bag filled with brown soft-peak icing, cut a small section from the tip of the piping bag and pipe the outlines of the cupcake cases. Fill the outlined sections with brown flooding icing and leave them to dry completely.

Once dry, use brown soft-peak icing to outline and decorate the cases.

Take a piping bag filled with yellow soft-peak icing, cut a small section from the tip of the bag and outline the icing on the cupcakes on a fifth of the cookies. Fill the outlined sections with yellow flooding icing. Leave them to set slightly, then sprinkle them with multicoloured sugar sprinkles.

Repeat for the remaining cookies, decorating an equal number with the pale pink, dark pink, blue and white icing. Leave them to dry completely.

Ghosts & Skeletons

**MAKES 20 GHOSTS &
12 SKELETONS**

INGREDIENTS

1 batch gingerbread cookies
(see page 9) in the shape of
ghosts (8 x 12cm)

1 batch chocolate cookies
(see page 8) in the shape of
gingerbread men (8 x 12cm)

600g royal icing (see page 56)

Black food colour

SPECIAL EQUIPMENT

Small electric drill with 3mm drill
bit for food use only

Thin orange satin ribbons

TIP

For the skeletons you could
buy plain gingerbread men and
then decorate them.

Prepare your paper piping bags (see page 57). Adjust the colour
(see page 56) and consistency of your royal icing (see pages
58 and 60). You will need soft-peak black and white icing and
flooding consistencies of white royal icing. Once prepared, keep
the piping bags in a re-sealable plastic bag to prevent the icing
from drying out between use.

Take a piping bag filled with white soft-peak icing, cut a small
section from the tip of the piping bag and pipe the outlines of
the ghosts. Fill the outlined sections with white flooding icing
and leave them to dry completely. Once dry, use black soft-peak
icing to pipe on the eyes and mouths of the ghost. You can also
use the black soft-peak icing to pipe cobwebs on some of the
ghosts. Leave them to dry completely.

To decorate the skeleton cookies, take the piping bag with
white soft-peak icing and pipe the outlines of a skeleton onto
each cookie. Fill the outlined sections with white flooding icing
and leave to dry completely.

Finally, make the ribbon holes in your ghost cookies (see page
7). Then thread pieces of thin orange satin ribbon through each
of the holes.

Ice Crystals

MAKES 6 OF EACH SIZE

INGREDIENTS

1 batch gingerbread cookies (see page 9) in various snowflake sizes and shapes: small (4cm diameter), medium (8cm diameter) and large (12cm diameter)

500g royal icing (see page 56)

Small amount of Superwhite Icing Whitener (optional)

Silver sugar balls

Prepare your paper piping bags (see page 57). Adjust the colour (see page 56) and consistency of your royal icing (see pages 58 and 60). You will need both soft-peak and flooding consistencies of white royal icing. You could also add a pinch of Superwhite Icing Whitener to the royal icing to ensure that it stays white when piped on top of the dark-coloured cookies. Once prepared, keep the piping bags in a re-sealable plastic bag to prevent the icing from drying out between use.

Take a piping bag filled with white soft-peak icing, cut a small section from the tip of the piping bag and pipe decorative details on all of the cookies. For larger sections of decoration, first outline with the white soft-peak icing and then fill with the white flooding icing.

To attach silver sugar balls to the cookies, pipe a dot of soft-peak icing onto the cookie and then place the sugar ball on top, gently pushing it into the royal icing. If necessary, use tweezers to drop the sugar balls in place.

Gingerbread House

INGREDIENTS

1 batch gingerbread cookie dough (see page 9) in the shape of a house: 8cm (width) x 12cm (height) x 10cm (depth)

Plain flour, for dusting

500g royal icing (see page 56)

SPECIAL EQUIPMENT

Gingerbread townhouse cutters and stencils available from Peggy Porschen or you can make your own (see page 62)

TIP

If you don't have stencils, you can pipe on the details of your house with soft-peak royal icing.

Place the dough on a lightly floured surface and briefly knead. Roll out the dough until it is about 5mm thick and cut it into the 6 pieces that make up the townhouse – 2 for the front and back (8 x 10cm), 2 for the sides (8 x 6cm) and 2 for the roof (10 x 7cm). Chill and then bake the gingerbread cookies as normal.

Adjust the consistency of half of the white royal icing to soft-peak (see page 58). Keep the icing in a bowl covered with a damp cloth to prevent it from drying out. Stencil your cookies (see page 62). Should the design look untidy you can clean it up with the tip of a small knife. Repeat for the remaining house shapes.

Assemble the house once the cookies have dried. Prepare a paper piping bag (see page 57) and fill it with white stiff-peak icing (see page 58). Lay the house pieces out with the designs facing down as if you were to unfold the 4 house walls. Cut a small section from the tip of the bag and pipe a thick line of royal icing along the vertical edges of the house front and back, then stick them together with the side wall pieces supporting them with your hands until they stand securely on their own. Let the walls set for at least 15 minutes. Pipe another thick line along the top edges of the side walls and stick the 2 roof pieces on top. Where they meet pipe some more icing and hold them in place until they stop sliding down. Let the house dry for at least 30 minutes.

Cut a larger hole at the tip of the piping bag and pipe a snail-trail line over the edges of the house – in addition to adding a decorative element, this helps to hide the joints and any royal icing that may have run out when sticking the pieces together.

Peggy's Pink Parlour

MAKES 2

INGREDIENTS

1 batch chocolate cookie dough
(see page 8) in the shape of
a house: 8cm (width) x 12cm
(height) x 8cm (depth)

Plain flour, for dusting

500g royal icing (see page 56)

Pink food colour

SPECIAL EQUIPMENT

Cake Parlour cutter and stencils
available from Peggy Porschen
or you can make your own (see
page 62)

TIP

If you don't have stencils, you can
pipe on the details of your house
with soft-peak royal icing.

Place the dough on a lightly floured surface and briefly knead.
Roll out the dough until about 3mm thick and cut it into the
5 pieces that make up the parlour – 2 for the front and back (8
x 12cm), 2 for the sides (8 x 12cm) and 1 for the roof (8 x 9cm).
Chill and then bake the chocolate cookies as normal.

Adjust the colour and consistency of half of the white royal icing
to pale pink soft-peak (see page 58). Keep the icing in a bowl
covered with a damp cloth to prevent it from drying out. Stencil
all your cookies (see page 62). Should the design look slightly
untidy you can clean it up with the tip of a small knife while the
icing is still wet. Repeat for the remaining parlour shapes.

Assemble the parlour once the cookies have dried. Prepare a
paper piping bag (see page 57). You will need 1 bag of pale
pink stiff-peak icing (see page 58). Cut a small section from the
tip of the bag and pipe a thick line of royal icing along the edges
of the cookies, then stick the pieces together.

Cut a larger hole at the tip of the piping bag and pipe a snail-
trail line over the edges of the parlour – in addition to adding a
decorative element, this helps to hide the joints and any royal
icing that may have run out when sticking the pieces together.

Christmas Jumpers

MAKES 25

INGREDIENTS

1 batch gingerbread cookies (see page 9) in the shape of tuxedos (8 x 10cm) or groom cutters available from Peggy Porschen

About 400g ivory sugar paste

2 tsp gum tragacanth

Small amount of white vegetable fat

Ivory, Christmas red, ice blue and holly green food colours

Edible glue

120g florist paste

SPECIAL EQUIPMENT

Wool texture mat

Dresden tool or small kitchen knife

Small and medium snowflake plunger cutters

Knead the sugar paste until smooth and pliable, adding the gum tragacanth and a small amount of white vegetable fat if it feels hard and brittle. Divide the paste into 4 parts. Keep 1 part ivory, then mix 1 part with red food colour, 1 part with blue food colour and 1 part with green food colour. Store the pastes in re-sealable plastic bags so they do not dry out between use.

Roll out the ivory sugar paste, until about 2mm thick and press the wool texture mat on top to emboss the knitted pattern. Use the tuxedo cookie cutter to cut out enough white jumpers to cover a quarter of the cookies and stick them on top with edible glue. Use the thin end of a Dresden tool to score lines on the cuffs, necks and hems of the jumpers. Repeat for the remaining cookies, decorating an equal number with the red, blue and green sugar pastes.

Knead the florist paste until smooth and pliable, adding a small amount of white vegetable fat if it feels hard and brittle. Divide the paste into 3 parts. Keep 1 part white, then mix 1 part with red food colour and 1 part with blue food colour. Roll out the paste until about 1mm thick. Cut out snowflakes of various colours with the snowflake cutters. Use edible glue to stick the snowflakes to the jumpers, trimming off any overhanging parts of the snowflakes if necessary.

Royal Icing

MAKES 1KG

INGREDIENTS

1kg icing sugar, sifted

Squeeze of lemon juice (optional)

4 egg whites or 25g Meri-White powdered egg white (mixed with water, as per the instructions on the packet)

COLOURING ROYAL ICING

Place the royal icing on a clean smooth surface or flat disc next to a small amount of paste or liquid food colour.

Use a palette knife to pick up a small amount of royal icing and mix it with the food colour. Work the food colour through the icing, making sure to break down any tiny specks of colour, which can burst and bleed as the icing dries if they are not properly incorporated. Once mixed, gradually add the coloured icing to the white icing and blend until you have achieved the required shade.

Place the icing sugar, lemon juice (if using) and three-quarters of the egg white or Meri-White in the clean and grease-free bowl of an electric mixer.

Mix on the lowest speed until well combined. You may want to cover the mixing bowl with a cloth to prevent the icing sugar from going everywhere. If the mixture looks too dry, add more egg white or Meri-White. The icing should look smooth, but not wet.

Scrape down the sides of the bowl after about 2 minutes to make sure the icing is well combined. If it still looks too dry and grainy along the edges, add a little more liquid.

If it looks slightly runny and glossy, add a little icing sugar to adjust the consistency.

Continue mixing on the lowest speed for 4–5 minutes, taking care to not overwork or over-aerate the mixture. The royal icing is ready when stiff peaks appear around the sides of the bowl and has a smooth and satin-like texture.

Transfer the royal icing to a clean bowl and cover with a damp cloth. The icing can be stored for up to 1 week at room temperature if covered with lid or cling film; or in the refrigerator if using fresh egg whites.

Making a Paper Piping Bag

Take a rectangular piece of waxed greaseproof paper or silicone paper – approximately 30 x 45cm – and cut it in half diagonally, from 1 corner to the opposite corner. To make a cleaner cut, slide the scissors through the paper rather than making a series of snips.

Hold 1 of the resulting triangles with the longest side at the top, the shortest side to the right and the right-angled corner at the bottom.

Bring the shorter corner down to the bottom corner, turning the paper over on itself to create a cone. With your left hand, wrap the longer corner twice around the cone. Ease the corner towards you so it joins together with the other 2 corners at the back of the cone.

Manipulate the innermost layer of paper where the 3 corners meet, pulling it towards you and to the left. Then pull the outermost layer of paper down towards you. Alternate these small movements until the cone forms a sharp point.

Fold the corners at the open end into the inside of the bag. Fold a second time to prevent unravelling.

Only ever half-fill a paper piping bag with royal icing because otherwise the contents will ooze out when you squeeze. Once filled, flatten the open end of the bag with the seam centred on one side. Fold over the 2 corners at the opening of the piping bag, then fold over the top of the bag and continue folding until you cannot fold any further; this creates tension that will make piping easier. Always fold away from the seam.

Store filled piping bags in re-sealable plastic bags until ready to use. When ready to pipe, snip off a small section straight across the top with sharp scissors.

Icing Techniques

ROYAL ICING CONSISTENCIES

The 3 useful consistencies of royal icing are stiff-peak icing, soft-peak icing and flooding icing. For soft-peak and flooding consistencies, you simply need to thin down your basic royal icing recipe with water, a little bit at a time, using a palette knife, until you have reached the right consistency. Always make sure you keep your icing in re-sealable bags when not using, to stop them from drying out.

STIFF-PEAK ICING CONSISTENCY
USED TO STICK COOKIES TOGETHER.

SOFT-PEAK ICING CONSISTENCY
USED TO PIPE OUTLINES, BORDERS AND DOTS.

FLOODING ICING CONSISTENCY
USED TO FILL IN THE CENTRE OF SPACES.

MAKING STIFF-PEAK ICING

Either use fresh royal icing on the day it is made, alternatively, place it into a small bowl and mix it through with a palette knife to loosen and aerate the mixture.

USING STIFF-PEAK ICING

Fill it into a piping bag and snip a slightly large tip off the front. Pipe along the areas of the cookies you would like to stick together.

MAKING SOFT-PEAK ICING

Dip the palette knife in water and mix it until the icing looks a little glossy. It should form peaks that fall over.

USING SOFT-PEAK ICING

Snip off a small tip of a filled piping bag. Hold the bag between your thumb and fingers; place your thumb over the folded end of the bag so it stays firmly closed, and place your index finger along the seam at the back of the bag. Use the index finger of your other hand to guide the nozzle.

To pipe lines, hold the bag at a 45° angle to the surface. Touch the starting point with the tip of the bag and slowly squeeze out the icing. As you are squeezing, lift up the bag about 2.5cm and guide the line. As you approach the end point of the line, gradually bring down the bag, stop squeezing and drop the line by touching the end point with the tip of the bag.

To pipe dots, hold the bag about 1mm above the surface and squeeze out the icing to create a dot. Keep the tip low inside the dot and allow the dot to spread to the required size, then stop squeezing and lift off the tip while flicking it in a circular motion. If the dot forms a little peak, flatten it with a damp brush.

techniques continued...

MAKING FLOODING ICING

Transfer the icing to a small bowl. Mix with a spatula and add a little water until the icing looks shiny, flows and flattens within 4–6 seconds. Tap the bowl onto a hard surface to bring any air bubbles to the top and prick them with a cocktail stick, before filling the icing into a piping bag.

USING FLOODING ICING

Snip off the tip of a filled piping bag and hold it in your preferred hand. To fill an area, start by flooding just within the soft-peak royal icing border and then continue moving in towards the centre. Be careful not to use too much flooding icing, as overfilling can cause the icing to leak and either run off the cookie or into a neighbouring colour.

When the entire area has been flooded, use a cocktail stick to push the royal icing into any corners or small sections it hasn't reached. If air bubbles form, you should pop them with a cocktail stick while the flooding icing is still wet.

ICING TIPS

• When icing cookies, always outline and flood 1 colour at a time, allowing the icing to dry completely before adding the next colour to the cookie – unless stated otherwise. This helps to prevent the different colours from bleeding into each other.

• Stronger colours tend to bleed if piped onto paler colours. To avoid bleeding, always ensure that the first colour has dried completely before decorating with the second colour.

• Outlines in stronger colours tend to be brittle and break more easily, so you should make the soft-peak consistency of these colours a little softer than usual. You should also avoid adding too much food colour where possible. For example, colour royal icing to a charcoal grey shade, which will look black once it dries.

• Flood thin and narrow areas while the outline is still wet, as this will reduce the risk of air pockets that may create holes in the surface when dry.

Stencil Techniques

1 Place the stencil on the surface of the cookie, holding it down at one end to prevent it from moving.

2 Use a palette knife to scoop up a small amount of soft-peak icing and spread a thin layer over the stencil, ensuring that all gaps are covered.

3 Carefully lift off the stencil and leave the iced cookie to dry. Repeat for the remaining cookies, cleaning the stencil between each use.

TIP

You can make your own stencils at home with a sheet of thick acetate or the see-through lid of a plastic container. Place the acetate or lid on top of a design template and cut out desired shapes or patterns with a craft knife.

Brush Embroidery Techniques

1 Take a piping bag filled with soft-peak icing and cut a small section from the tip of the piping bag. Working from the background to the foreground, pipe the outline of 1 petal at a time.

2 Use a slightly damp paintbrush to pull through a midpoint in the line. Always pull the paintbrush from the edge to the centre, mimicking the natural grain of the petal. Try to not break the outer line as this will distort the shape. If you want to create more definition with your brush strokes, slightly dry the paintbrush and flatten it. Pull the paintbrush through the icing on the thinner edge.

3 Continue creating the petals 1 at a time, then allow the entire layer to dry. Each layer of petals must dry before you pipe on the next layer in order to give the blossom a 3-dimensional finish.

Acknowledgements

Creating and writing this little book of joy has been an awful lot of fun! The most thanks go to the fantastic people I have worked with. Thank you to my brilliant team at PP: Stephanie, Tory and Alexia for helping with the concept, creation and editorial of this wonderful book. You all are so incredibly talented and have done such a fantastic job! Thank you Georgia Glynn Smith, for the ever beautiful photography, and Rebecca Newport for your quirky take on styling. It's been very inspirational working with you both. A big thank you goes to my publishing team at Quadrille for their continued enthusiasm, hard work and support. Jane O'Shea, Gemma Hogan, Helen Lewis, Lisa Pendreigh and Romilly Morgan, thank you ever so much for yet another beautiful project.

Editorial director **Jane O'Shea**
Creative director **Helen Lewis**
Editor **Romilly Morgan**
Designer **Gemma Hogan**
Photographer **Georgia Glynn Smith**
Stylist **Rebecca Newport**
Props **Talking Tables, Brighton Beautiful**
Production director **Vincent Smith**
Production controller **Aysun Hughes**

First published in 2014 by
Quadrille Publishing Ltd
www.quadrille.co.uk

British Library Cataloguing-in-Publication Data
A catalogue record for this book is available from the
British Library.

ISBN: 978 184949 497 7

Printed in China

**A selection of the cutters, stencils and moulds used
in this book are available from peggyporschen.com**

**The cookie dimensions in the book all use the
formula width x height.**